How

How to Become Live Audio Mixer

7 Secrets of a Hollywood Live Audio Mixer Who Does LIVE EVENTS Every Month!

HowExpert with Mike Napoli

For more tips related to this topic, visit HowExpert.com/liveaudiomixer.

Recommended Resources

- HowExpert.com – Quick 'How To' Guides on All Topics from A to Z by Everyday Experts.
- HowExpert.com/free – Free HowExpert Email Newsletter.
- HowExpert.com/books – HowExpert Books
- HowExpert.com/courses – HowExpert Courses
- HowExpert.com/clothing – HowExpert Clothing
- HowExpert.com/membership – HowExpert Membership Site
- HowExpert.com/affiliates – HowExpert Affiliate Program
- HowExpert.com/writers – Write About Your #1 Passion/Knowledge/Expertise & Become a HowExpert Author.
- HowExpert.com/resources – Additional HowExpert Recommended Resources
- YouTube.com/HowExpert – Subscribe to HowExpert YouTube.
- Instagram.com/HowExpert – Follow HowExpert on Instagram.
- Facebook.com/HowExpert – Follow HowExpert on Facebook.

Table of Contents

STEP 1: Learn the Standards of Audio Mixing

Basics of Working With Microphones

- When working with talent such as singers and bands, the first step to get a great and controllable mix is getting the equipment in the right spot for the specific venue. The equipment refers to mainly microphones and speakers. The Speakers should be as close to the audience as practical. This means a speaker should never be 10 inches away from the closest audience member's ear and should not be 100 feet away either. It should be in a practical place that still sounds appealing, (these people will understand that it will still be very loud in the front) and the main rule of thumb is to seriously use common sense.
- That is the biggest rule in mixing. Along with keeping that in mind, your next objective is to get the microphones as close to the source as practical. No microphone should be shoved in someone's mouth or guitar amp, but also shouldn't be 10 feet away. For pretty much everything, the closer the mic is to the source then the better it sounds unless it just sounds awful or not right which in that case, use common sense and experiment with slightly different positions of the microphone. Whether

that is the case or not you must always understand where to start.

- The reason to get the mic as close to the source as practical is to obtain the most acoustic frequencies and gain as possible. Low frequencies like bass or the "soul" in people's voices are omnidirectional meaning that they like to spread out and be heard in different directions. This is why you can be leaving the club at night and still hear the bass but not all the high frequencies since the high frequencies are inside going one direction and the bass is going everywhere in almost equal amounts. High frequencies are the opposite and are unidirectional which can make them be heard from farther away if directed right at your ear or mic. So these concepts impact what the microphone hears.

- The farther you get away from the source the faster low frequencies get lost compared to high frequencies. This is because the mic is still pointed at the source where the high frequencies are moving straight at it and the low frequencies have spread out now. Along with this, the microphone will clearly not be as powerful and catch everything forcing you, the mixer, to have to run everything hot (very loud) putting yourself at risk of feedback or ranging dynamics of loudness with the unpredictable talent moving the mic. Lastly on the mixing board, whichever channel the microphone is plugged into (how to plug in the microphone will be explained in step 2) there will be a fader assigned to that channel. The fader is the slider that goes up and down. It controls the volume just like the knob on your car's radio and it goes from as low as infinity which is silent to +10dB usually. "0" or what is called "unity" is where you want to try your best and have your fader live for your average show volume. But if you start from infinity and turn up the volume to -30dB (which will be -30dB away from 0, very quiet) and the mic is already too loud then how do you fix this? Well there will be an attribute knob on every mixing board called either "Gain" or "Trim" and what this does is change the attenuation of the channel it is assigned to by making the mic louder or quieter and in turn making it more sensitive or less sensitive. Think of it as another fader, and if you have the gain at the right level then you should be able to have your fader live at unity.

• So if the mic is too loud at -30dB then turn down the gain knob and put up the fader until you reach unity. If you can't get the mic loud enough then turn up the gain. Be careful with turning up the gain too much as that makes the microphone more sensitive and leaves it more vulnerable to feedback. If feedback occurs and you cannot get the fader to unity don't stress over it. The reason why you want the fader at unity is because it makes it much easier to make smaller volume adjustments, but it is not the end of the world if you cannot reach this goal for a particular reason. Understanding this concept will allow you as the Mixer to know what to listen for in different mic positions and how to control its volume. (feedback will be explained later)

Basics of Acoustics

- When Mixing Audio of any sort it is often not a relevant thought to many listeners of just how much goes into that work of art to make it sound the best it can. The main goal of any mixer is to get a sound from the source that sounds natural. Nothing should stand out and everything should be crisp and clear just like how you would want it as a regular listener. In Live Mixing this is never an easy task however. Acoustics of the environment a Mixer is working in is the second step to finding the right mix after proper placement of speakers and microphones. If the space the event is held in is a large open space with very hard parallel walls, sound will bounce off all these walls at an incredible rate taking a long time to dissipate and overall sounding like a big mess. This is called reverberation and can easily be heard by just clapping in a space such as this. It will take a while for the sound to fade away and with singers, a full band, and an audience nothing is going to be distinct and heard. Keeping that large example in mind, the opposite of a space like that will give a flat dead feeling to the room with no dynamics. The room can still be big (but harder to control) and will have walls or padding that are very soft and fluffy easily absorbing sound not letting it bounce back for the listener to hear. This is a much better space for any Mixer as it now gives him/her the control of what the space will sound like instead of fighting it. If a space feels too dead and doesn't have any feeling then there are effects inside certain mixing boards that you can use to give the feeling of real dynamics in a room. Reverb which is a digital representation that is controllable reverberation is one effect that is used very often in just about all of music. Keeping all this in mind when getting ready before the event, you should play your favorite song that you know word for word and sound for sound at show volume in the venue. Then walk around the venue and just listen to how different the song sounds. Is it clustered and messy? Is it too bassy? Or is there no feel to it and not enough bass? Listening to this will get you ready to know what to listen for and just how much the acoustic space you are working in is going to impact your sound. Once you go through that you should then get yourself a microphone and speak through it saying "one" for bass notes and "two" for higher notes. This will tell you how your microphones are picking up in the space and how they are reacting to it as well.

Basics of Equalizing a Singer's Voice

- Now whether the space is bad or good, a mixer has the ability to mix and EQ (equalize) sounds. If someone gets on the mic and starts singing (mic in right position) and they sound really deep and muddy, almost unclear in what they are saying then that means that there is too much low end in their voice to sound natural through the speakers. On every mixing board there is an EQ page or labeled knobs that allow you to reduce or gain the volume of specific frequencies. So if someone sounds like this example then the best thing to do is take away some low frequencies. Keep in mind that the audible range for humans is 20 Hz to 20'000 Hz or 20 kHz. (20 Hz is very low and 20 kHz is very high) Keep going until you find a sound you like. If you reduce low frequencies like 200Hz and it still doesn't sound natural then just slowly change the frequency to 250Hz, 300Hz, 350Hz etc until it sounds natural.

The same concept applies for people that sound shrill, either taking away some high frequencies or adding some lows and even finding a combination between the two. Something to keep in mind when going through and using EQs on all the microphones is to always try and take away or reduce frequencies than add. When reducing it is much more controlled and will make the mix sound cleaner as opposed to pushing frequencies louder and trying to make them stand out. Also when raising the volume of frequencies, that will make the overall volume of the mic be louder and more sensitive. You do not want to make the microphone so sensitive that it distorts and sounds awful, and when the mic is louder there is a stronger chance of feedback. (Common frequency problems in people's voices are between 1 kHz to 2 kHz if they sound too harsh) Later on there will be more information about how much equalizing can help in different situations.

STEP 2: Learn How to Set Up All the Speakers and Microphones to the Board

Plugging in Microphones to the Board

- Now that you understand the basic ideas of how to get a good sound from your mix, you must be able to hook up your equipment to hear the new skills and knowledge you now have! The first step is to make a list and be as organized as possible. Many people working in this industry get caught up in the stress of a fast paced event and do not stay organized making more work for themselves in the end. The ones staying organized are the ones that succeed. So first find out info from the event coordinator and bands of how many instruments or people there are which will allow you to know how many microphones and other equipment is needed.

Then once this is known, write down all the inputs (mics and anything else that needs a connection to the board from the talent) on a piece of paper. This is called you Input List. On this list write down the corresponding info of what mic and channel that instrument will go to. So if you write down Singer 1 - SM58 Mic - Channel 1 then that means that singer 1 will have an SM58 Mic with an XLR cable (all mics use this cable) that goes from the mic to the board into input 1 which will then allow the mic to be controlled on channel 1 of the board. Do this for every single input you have written down and then you will be ready for the band to come, and already be mentally prepared for what to do.

Now along with this, there may be an called a Snake Box back stage. These are very normal to see in every venue and it is just an extension of a bunch of XLR cables going from backstage to the board so you do not have to personally run 50 cables yourself. To identify one you should see a lot of XLR inputs on a box with a fat cable going out to the Front of House. To use this, writing down where things should be plugged in is critical. An example of what to write down is: Singer 1 - SM58 Mic - Snake Box Channel 1 - Board Channel 1. Always take your time plugging into the Snake Box as many times people will plug into the channel below or above the channel they intended creating big problems later on. As you can probably realize, the numbers can get switched around a lot especially in the heat of the moment so once again it is extremely important to be organized.

Plugging in Speakers to the Board

- At this point you should have an input list created and now before the band or talent even shows up your main objective should be to get all the speakers functioning properly. There are many different types of speakers but the main thing to look for is if they are passive or active.

Passive means that they will require an amplifier of some sort to give them the power needed to even be "turned on" basically. An active speaker will have an amplifier built into the speaker and will have a regular IEC/AC power cable that comes with it and just plugs into a wall circuit. Wherever you have to get your power from, it is the same concept for both.

• The active speaker gets power from a regular outlet and a passive goes through an amp which goes to an outlet. The cables for a passive speaker are usually Speakon cables which have a circular shape and just go right from the speaker into the amp. Then out of the amp there are XLR input ports which will take an XLR that comes from the board the the amp. Or on an active speaker it will go straight into the speaker which will have a XLR input port. From the board though, a speaker is not an input like a microphone. There is no music being picked up by the speaker that goes into the board. It is the exact opposite, the board has all these inputs from mics which it will then output to a speaker so that the speaker is receiving audio and makes it heard.

• So at the board there is a lot of different lingo used for outputs but the main ones are called AUX. (if it doesn't say AUX it should say output somewhere) The AUX have an XLR or Quarter Phone cable output. These cables are compatible so if you have an adapter for the cable to fit into the output then it will work perfect if you run into this problem. Once the speaker is plugged into the AUX let's say AUX

1, then whatever inputs are being sent into AUX 1 on the board will go out to that speaker. On the board you should find either knobs that say AUX 1 or there will be a fader page that says AUX.

- If there is a knob then whatever channel the knob is over, for instance channel 1 with our singer, the more you turn that knob and send channel 1 to AUX 1 then the louder the singer will get in that speaker. If there is a fader page then all the faders will change positions and it will say that you are on the AUX 1 page. Now any fader you slide up you will increase the volume of that input being sent to AUX 1. This is used for many speakers. For your main speakers there will be an outport on the board that says "stereo out" plug the XLRs from the speakers into these. Now your regular faders on your analog board that control the volume of channels and your home page faders on your digital board will determine the volume sent to the stereo mix. Same concept as the AUX but with the main speakers.

Cables

- Now last step for your setup is knowing about your cables. No Mixer wants to be stuck in a position relating to cables that he/she knows nothing about. Without cables your microphones and your speakers don't work which leaves you out of a job. The main reason to know cables is to know what to use based on what the equipment requires. The second is to know what to do when something isn't working. After creating your input list (before you are at the event) you should have an idea of exactly how much cable needs to be used and what types of cables and adapters that are needed.

- If you show up to the gig and you forgot the one adapter needed, then part of the show can be messed up at fault of you. XLR cables are the main cables used in audio. Now there are different types of XLR cables though. There are the three pin that are the main ones used and most common. There are the four pin which are fairly uncommon and typically used for equipment that both has a microphone and a speaker like a Clear Com, (Radio used in the industry) and lastly there are five pin XLRs. So make sure that the right ones are used for the right equipment. Next, there are Quarter Phone cables which are mentioned above. These are basic guitar cables and are very common.

- Most keyboardist have an amp that need to use this cable and drum pads too. There are two different types of Quarter Phone cables, balanced and unbalanced. An unbalanced only has one ring on the tip of the cable and works fine but won't cancel out any electrical hum getting picked up through the cable from amps, power, or any other electrical disturbance. A balanced one with two rings on the tip will do that and give you a higher chance of less problems for the most part, but both are great.

- Next is the mini stereo or 3.5mm cable which is just like the Quarter Phone but smaller. Known in today's society as the aux cord for our phones. The same rules apply for the mini stereo cable as Quarter Phones in terms of balanced and unbalanced. The last main one is RCA cable which are most known for older TVs with the Red White and Yellow cables. In audio it is just Red and White for right and left audio. These can be used for certain cheaper amps or mixer inputs and other things too. They are useful to have but not always practical to use as they are not the best quality and not dependable. Understanding the difference and uses of these cables will make a Mixer into a true engineer of not only sound but allowing one to set up the entire stage the correct way without issues and get the sound that he/she wants.

STEP 3: Getting the right mix

Feedback and Equalizing

1. Now that your speakers are working, and the
    equipment is all plugged in located in a
    practical spot it is now time to make the show
    your own through mixing. This is the fun part
    of the job but also very fast paced so you must
    be prepared and understand what to listen for.
    One of the biggest problems in any live event
    whether it be a band, a musical, or just a large
    conference with a PA setup there is always the
    possibility of feedback which was mentioned
    earlier in STEP 1. Feedback is any Mixer's
    worst enemy and is the most noticeable thing
    in any event besides equipment failure.
    Feedback is when the source reaches the
    microphone which then the mic amplifies that
    sound to the board and out through the
    speakers, and if the speaker is close enough or
    loud enough that the microphone picks up
    what is coming out of the speaker then the mic
    repeats what it just picked up a second ago.
    Now the speaker is outputting again what the
    mic has just picked up even louder and then
    the cycle repeats. This happens so fast in audio
    that there isn't even a noticeable delay or echo
    in what is being picked up. Instead it cycles so
    fast that it becomes an expenential growing
    hum from the speakers at whatever frequency
    is being picked up the most. So if a high
    pitched violin mic feedbacks then the feedback

will be a high pitched hum almost like a dog whistle but much louder and audible to the human ear. If a bass mic feeds back then the feedback will be an earthquake type of hum. Now that you know what to listen for it is time to fix it. First just bring down the volume of the microphone in the corresponding speaker that is having the feedback issues. Just by lowering the volume on a channel fader by 5dB the feedback will go away. Next check to see where the mic and speakers are placed, if everything is okay, but you still can't hear that microphone then you are able to EQ and reduce the frequency of what the microphone is picking up or what the speaker is putting out. As mentioned before you can EQ any channel and if you can hear that it is a low hum then a great idea would be to reduce the volume of that frequency in that mic. Now you can turn up the volume again on the mic, but the low frequency will still be reduced not causing feedback. Or if multiple mics are having the same problem with same speaker or speakers then you can EQ the Stereo Output (if those are the speakers that are having the issues) or any AUX channel on many boards. (Some analog boards unfortunately do not have an EQ for AUX outputs so you will have to go through input channels instead and EQ microphones)

Balancing Volumes

1. No feedback errors means a clean show and after you have your EQ on your speakers and inputs to make everything sound natural, next is actually mixing volumes of channels which is done with the faders on the board. This is where things are sometimes very simple or can be very tricky and will change in every event. The main goal is to make everything sound natural in volume. The band should be tight and sound like the record. Drums shouldn't be blaring loud with a quiet guitar and the bass player shouldn't be rumbling the stage on a sweet ballad. So the best thing to do is to really listen and keep everything sounding unified that honestly sounds good to you. Once you get to this point of everything sounding good, you should make sure that everything as a whole is at an appropriate volume. The venue shouldn't be lifeless and also shouldn't make people deaf. These things are simple and require patience, practice, and especially common sense. The more you do this with anything the more you know what the average ear expects. But once you get that great mix your job is not at all over yet. Throughout the day or night people will be moving all over with their mics, musicians will play naturally a little softer or a lot harder, certain moments of an event will want dynamics and are meant to be soft and others are meant to be strong, and musicians may have solos. So you should always have your hands on the faders and make slight adjustments to keep the perfect mix in tact and

create dynamics of your own for the softer parts of a performance and stronger parts too. This is what makes it your performance as well, and how you are able to change the feel to every song or speech makes it your own work of art.

Using Dynamics

- The last main part of getting a good mix is controlling sound before it happens. On every digital board there will be dynamics called compressors and expanders/gates. A compressor allows you to set a threshold and once the volume of the mic reaches that threshold the compressor will hold back the audio from getting too loud. So if someone randomly screams in a Musical you won't blow out any speakers or ears. The threshold should be set to where it doesn't take effect in talking and once there is singing/screaming it begins to take effect. The "ratio" on a compressor is just how hard it compresses the audio once the threshold is reached. (a 1:1 ratio is the weakest and a 8:1 ratio is extremely high) Practice with compressors and always aim for a smooth sound where the compressor is not noticeable to the crowd. An expander/gate is the opposite. This can be used to quiet breathing and unwanted small sounds. You set the threshold of the expander and until that threshold is passed with the audio coming in nothing will come out of the speakers. It is best advised to use an extremely low threshold for anything as you will cut out main lines of dialogue since people might talk loud for a second passing the threshold of your expander, but then speak quietly which will be muted from the expander. Your compressor is your strongest friend as it helps control loud sounds before they happen. Plus a compressor has what is called "Make Up Gain" or "Output" which allows you to raise the volume of the channel essentially giving you another way to mix volume. It is not like gain and won't make your microphone necessarily more sensitive but will make the channel itself louder. With this idea you can mix with a compressor and have most of the board working for you instead of fighting the actors and their intense dynamics. If you have a digital board 99% of the time there will not be any of these controls. If you wish to use these you can buy physical boxes with gates and compressors and put that into the insert hole of any channel. An example would be a DBX Compressor which are very well known and used with lots of analog boards. To know if you have mixed a great show at the end of every performance or speech then you will be an unknown figure to every person in the crowd. They will think that the band sounded amazing, everything was so clear and easy to hear, and will make them go home knowing that they have witnessed a great performance, speech, play ect. Your job as the mixer is to make the talent sound the best they can and allow the opportunity to have the best sounding show for every audience member. If things sound off and wrong or there are equipment issues then everyone in the audience will blame the mixer. So if things go right you will be a hidden shadow in the minds of everyone. If it sounds like you as the mixer won't get credit for a great job then you are wrong! Everyone on stage, the talent, crew, and all other people working in the business will hear what you have created and will give you the appreciation you deserve. This is where you will get the contacts you will want, and get you the shows you desire to mix.

STEP 4: Communicate with the Talent and Crew

Communication with Band

1. One of the biggest steps for any Mixer is the ability to work with the talent. This is what separates a good Mixer from a great one and will give you the edge to any competition in your shows. Working with talent is not as easy as everyone thinks though due to the vast variety of personalities you'll meet. In this industry it is a fast paced environment with problems constantly arising, and the talent does not have time for problems. By forming a relationship with the talent as the mixer they will not only feel comfortable with you, but also you will be able to fix the problems that may happen later through communication. Two minds testing and going through setup/sound check will absolutely find more problems and fix them quicker. If a problem occurs for any of the talent while on stage during a show they will very easily take the dirty looks they are receiving from their co-stars and pass them on to the tech crew. You must be able to assess the situation, calm it down by communicating, and be able to fix it. This is very challenging in high stress situations and you must understand that in the business when you are yelled at the talent is not yelling at you specifically, they're yelling because there is a problem and you

happen to be there. They will greatly appreciate your help once the issue is fixed but you must not take any of the things said to heart. If you do, this business will tear you down. When in a situation like this, by communicating, being prepared, and being confident in your abilities you will be able to counter any problems that happen during a show or rehearsal.

Always Be Positive

1. Working on any show, you will obviously be with a person a lot through the span of the event whether it's one day or longer. Keeping this in mind it is especially important to keep a good attitude and good relationships with the people you are seeing constantly. Don't hold a grudge from a problem that happened before with anyone. This can be easily achieved if you don't take everything to heart but rather learn from it and fix it as mentioned above. But if you do hold a grudge, it will drastically change how you work and people work around you. People will not communicate as much with you leading to more problems and you getting more frustrated. This is why it is never healthy for the show when you're not in your best working condition. Once relationships between talent and crew are sealed in a bad way, problems will compound faster than ever leaving the show a mess for you and the talent. Always keep your relationships in a good state in order for you to be the best you can, and for the show to run the

best it can. Apart of keeping a good relationship and not getting into a position where you or anyone else is upset is to be positive everyday. Coming to the show positive will make the people around you connect with you more and work better with you. By keeping this state of mind and understanding that not everything is personal, you should be just fine in the department of communicating with the talent.

Communication with Crew

1. Last is communicating with the crew. This is just as important as with the talent as you are all in the same boat. Many will be your lifeline when something goes wrong and you all have a respect for what each other do. These ideas sound like common sense, (the most important thing for a Mixer) but are easily forgotten in the stress of this industry. Never disrespect someone and their job. This is an instant knife in your relationship and the relationship of the crew around you. Also never take over someone else's job in the sense that you feel that it can be done better and you start hovering over them giving them your ideas of what to do. It never hurts to give some of your own input, but you must respect the fact that it is their position to work on that job on that show. On the flip side you must always be open to criticism from the crew around you too. Take it positively and into consideration, learn from

what others have in their own experiences. Along with this, you must be independent when working in this industry and with the crew. Take initiative when working on tasks together and get your job done instead of standing around waiting to be told what to do. If you need the crew or the talent to do something for you as the Mixer then you must speak up. Speakers, input list, mics, cables, and sound checks don't just get setup and begin on their own. This is the Mixer's job to make sure that everything is being taken care of and being efficiently worked on in order for the show to start on time. This is all about communication and will show your crew, talent, and producers that you understand what you're doing and absolutely love what you do.

STEP 5: Networking and Promoting

Networking

1. Along with communication with the talent, crew, and producers throughout the show, you're next goal is to network with all the people you meet. This is why it is absolutely crucial to communicate properly and create a relationship with every person you work with. As a Live Audio Mixer you will most likely not have a straightforward job or be guaranteed a show every month paying top dollar. You will get your gigs through self marketing, but more so through the people you meet. Word of mouth is your strongest tool in getting more gigs. The more your name is out in the industry the more calls you will get from people you've worked with, and from people you've never spoken to but have gotten your info from someone that you've worked with. This industry is all about who you know and what makes it very different from others as this is what you will have to rely on at times. It is rare, but there will be times you may meet a crew member that has a better gig than you but is awful at their art. Whether it be they do not care, do not practice, or it is not their thing they just aren't fit for the job. But the way they have gotten where they are is through the people they know! If the whole band only

knows one drummer then guess who will be getting the drummer spot whether or not they are good. You must as a Mixer, or anything in this industry for that matter, be willing and able to network and get your name out there through other people. From experience, this is where 99% of your jobs will come from and how you will get the shows you desire. Along with making connections, do not only think of getting your info out, but make sure you get info from the people you work with too. This will help people feel comfortable getting your info and respect you more, and in turn giving you a higher chance of getting gigs. This leads to promoting yourself, the bigger your résumé of shows you've worked on, the better chances you have to promote yourself.

Self Promotion

1. Next is self marketing and promotion. Getting yourself out there into the world of show business all by yourself can seem extremely daunting especially when just beginning without connections and experience. The fact of the matter is that it is daunting and it is okay to be nervous, but you must try! Nobody becomes successful without the hard work that is necessary. To begin, a great way to start is by creating an online presence. There are many services that allow you to create you own website either for free or a very small price including sites like Wix, Weebly, or even

WordPress. This will allow you when you meet people or are exchanging info to give them something more than just a name and number without any real background. This will give them exactly what you want them to see on your own site. Along with that, these sites will allow you the opportunity to be found online which does the job for you! After your site, social media is your next stop. Make a professional page that has a bio explaining who you are and what you love to do. This can be done on Facebook, Twitter, or Instagram preferably as they are extremely popular and natural for people to have and follow you. On your pages you should begin documenting through photos and such what you are working on giving you a growing résumé that builds itself for you as you work. Next is finding ways to explain the type of services you can provide to people and one of the biggest best places to do this is through Craigslist. Putting up an ad explaining what you can provide will help tons of people find you without you doing the hard work! And then on your social media pages you are able to promote your own website and Craigslist ads so people can see for themselves what you can provide. Next there are sites that promote freelancers and help them propose themselves to people who need services from workers that are professional in specific things. Upwork and Freelancer are very well known and amazing websites to get started with this. And lastly after making your online presence known and beginning to have it work for you, you need to go out in person to production companies that work in this industry as a business. In Hollywood there is Ratt Audio, 3rd Encore, and Morning Star to name a few. Look online in your area to see what is around you! By applying at these businesses you give yourself the best chance possible to break through and begin to make a name for yourself. A lot of these businesses will not pay well if at all and are lots of work, but if you love what you do this is starts your experience, self marketing, and networking leading to many great opportunities.

Keeping Connections Over Time

1. Last with networking and marketing is being able to keep the same relationship with the people that have helped to get you more gigs in your career. Everyone you know in this industry is an asset in your arsenal and you cannot afford to lose any of those if you wish to be successful. After a perfect show this is the most important action for any Mixer and it applies not only to the one who has gotten you to the gig, but also the people working on the gig that have helped you in any way. Following this will allow you to not only be remembered by these people, but to be wanted again for more shows by these people. One of the most important things that is often forgotten through the excitement and stress of this type of work is to show your gratitude and thanks to the people that helped you get there. This is so easily forgotten whether you believe it or not,

and it is why it is in this guide. You must always give your thanks to the people that got you where you are on the event you are working on, and many times you will get gigs from a person that is not even working on the event themselves. In this situation you should thank them for the opportunity before the show actually begins and then invite them to the event in a cordial manner making them feel not only appreciated, but like they are respected. Along with this, after the show has officially completed whether it is a few weeks or just one night you should take the time to thank them once again and explain how great the experience was. The most important part of this is to let them know that if they ever need an extra hand in any show or are looking for a Mixer, then call any time! You love working with this group of people and that it has been a pleasure. This will lock in that relationship with that person and leave you off on a great note leading to future gigs. It seems simple, (using common sense once again) but it will give you the best opportunity for more gigs and keep your relationships in tact.

STEP 6: Tips in the Industry

Jobs You May Get

1. When you begin in this industry you first have
    to understand and realize that you may not
    begin in your favorite Front of House mixing
    position. You will get offered gigs as a
    stagehand or monitor mixer if you're lucky.
    Unfortunately monitor mixing can be one of
    the most stressful jobs in show business and is
    also one of the most important if not the most
    important job in the industry. The reason for
    this is that you are now in control of what the
    band hears. By mixing monitors you are mixing
    only the speakers that are on stage placed for
    the band. Today many bands are beginning to
    switch to in ear monitors which are the same
    principle but just like ear buds in their ear
    which you can mix. When in this position you
    will be yelled at by the band and you have to be
    quick and listen to whatever they say so that
    they can get the right mix. When doing
    monitors you will put all the inputs in your
    board (the same as explained in step 2) and
    then all your outputs can go through AUX for
    individual speakers or in ear monitors for each
    band member. If there is a monitor mixer
    which there is for all concerts, there will be a
    splitter for all the inputs from the band. So
    instead of plugging in the XLR straight from
    the mic to the board, it will go into the splitter.
    Then from the splitter there will normally be a

33

Snake Cable that will go to your board with all the input cables being extended for you to plug in. And then there will be another Snake Cable to run the the Front of House Mixer and his or her board. This is how both boards get the inputs they need. You do not have to do this for your monitors on stage however because only you are mixing those and he will be mixing the main speakers. You must put a limiter on each AUX channel if you are able to depending on boards as this will make sure if there is any sudden loud noise it will limit how loud it gets so that it doesn't blow out the talents ears. The limiter should be set no higher than a 2:1 ration so that it doesn't impact anything but loud sudden noises. Also when working with EQs for monitors you should be aiming to only have a flat sound, not an incredible powerful sound. Lastly, use the monitor out on your board which will allow you to have your own in ear monitor or speaker so that you can solo the AUX channels and when mixing a band member you can hear exactly what he or she hears. The principle and concept of mixing monitors is fairly simple, but the stress will be from the band members themselves as they want their mix a specific way right away. If you can work with the band's tech guys they will usually help you out in giving you an idea of what they want and get your sound check just right so that when show time comes you just have to make small adjustments. During the show you have to either be staring at the band ready for any cue to make adjustments or already me making adjustments. If this job is the one offered then you must take this job as the people that succeed and have experience in this field are the ones that become the next Front of House Mixer. Also offered is the stagehand position. Normally this job is fairly simple, and just like mixing monitors you are backstage for the entire show. Your main job in this position is to assist anyone who needs it in setting up the stage before the talent comes, then help set up the band with the specific microphones and begin to run cable following the input list from either one of the Mixers. Once everything is set up on stage including the band, the show begins and your job is to help out and fix whatever goes wrong. If a cable is defective you have to go out on stage, act professional, and get that cable swapped out as efficiently as possible. At the end of the night you will be breaking down everything (which almost everyone helps out with unless it's a huge production) and will have very long hours. This is a huge part of anyone's career as it gives you insight on all the jobs that you assist with during set up and gives you the ability to connect and network with tons of people. As you do this you will build a relationship with not only your crew members but also the people that hired you and they will begin asking of more jobs from you in a department that you excel in which is sound. It is important to take any job you can get as it leads to opportunities you would have never thought of before.

Mixing Tips

- Often when mixing you will quickly find out that who ever has hired you is closely listening and watching you. The reason for this is to make sure that their show is going to be ran the way they envision. This is natural for people to do with something that they are creating and you should not feel nervous or bad about this. Keeping that in mind, after a rehearsal or even a show they will talk to you and may sometimes give their opinion on a given issues of theirs with your mixing. For example: you are in a 99 seat theater and with a band of 9, full drums included so you are pushing the microphones to be audible and heard over the band. Then the producer says, "It sounds too loud in here" to you. Now this is tricky because you will soon realize that people without experience and knowledge in your line of work either don't know how to explain in comprehensive terms what they mean or do not understand that a certain situation is inevitable. When in this situation you must greatly take into consideration what they are saying and freely express your deep concern for the issue. Then depending on if it is true or even fixable, you need to explain to them how you understand, will work on fixing it, and the science of why it is occurring. From experience this will work. They will know that you understand the issue, know why it is happening, and especially that you will try your best to fix the problem. So for this example you will have to explain that a full band in this type of space is going to be extremely loud due to the fact that it is so condense making the actors having to fight to be heard. This is a very difficult and delicate situation that you are working on and will need to talk to the both the band and actors together to find an appropriate level for both and get a tameable volume. With this type of mature explanation you should be alright and you must follow suit with what you have said. Never make the producer or whomever it is feel like he or she doesn't know what they are talking about. This will very quickly ruin your networking and give yourself a bad name. The same thing goes for musicians as well. In the industry you will quickly learn that musicians have a reputation of not being the most friendliest. This is not true for every musician, however a great majority of them expect everything to be perfect in their set up right away. (This is why mixing monitors is very stressful as mentioned above)

Always Stay Productive

- One of the most important things, especially when first starting in this business is always staying productive. On any event there is never time to relax and just mingle unless you are on break (if you're lucky enough to get one) or if you have completed all your tasks before call time for the show. This is so rare and you will realize that if you are doing your job right you will often not have any relax time at all from preparation to call time and striking the stage after the show. If people begin to see that you are not working then you will be judged very quickly ruining your chances of networking, and the only way to hopefully get back your reputation is by putting on an amazing show which isn't so easy when everything isn't completed. If you are running sound, lighting, producing, directing etcetera then you will find it fairly easy to keep busy as there is so much to do. But when you are a stagehand, the position you typically get at entry level and the one that will launch your career if worked properly, then you will find it a little more difficult to stay busy. If the band hasn't arrived and everyone is working on their own tasks then what do you do? Start asking around if people need help and just use common sense once again. If no one needs help then check all the connections, make sure everything is show ready, clean up all things present to the audience, and focus on being productive. This is the type of attitude the people higher up than you look for and the way that you will get more gigs through your self promotion and networking. No one wants to hire someone and pay them good money for them to not be productive. Make yourself the valuable asset that you can be. Now if you aren't a stagehand and are for some reason still having issues of staying busy as a Mixer then always check everything. Your speakers should be checked every so often to make sure nothing has glitched out or been moved accidentally. If you have wireless microphones you must alway check your batteries and check that all your connections are coming through properly through the levels on your board. When working live events you will learn that no matter how much you prepare you just will never get to every problem before it happens so the more you check everything the higher your chances are of running a successful show.

STEP 7: Always Keep Practicing and Never Give Up

Keep Practicing

1. Now that you understand the basics of Live Audio Mixing and know what it takes to succeed in this industry, you are ready to take on the real world and use your knowledge that you've learned to do what you love. The only thing this How to Guide can't teach is true experience which is where you will learn the most and become the best.

2. However you are never done learning and and getting better. Often times people just beginning do not know what to really listen for. But the best thing about working with Audio is that it is not just music. It is all of sound referring to, acoustic space, music, speech, equipment, natural noise, city noise, and much more! You are constantly surrounded by what you do for a living and what you love. You must practice and develop your ears to the best they can be and the best way to achieve this is just by listening!

3. When you listen to a fan in the room, identify the different frequencies that it is producing. Listen for the subtle difference of it. Hear how the fan sounds based on the environment of the room and what type of effect the acoustic space has. When you listen to someone speak do the same thing since this is what you will be

mixing! When you listen to music whether it is live, through headphones, or just on a speaker you must listen for what stands out and what blends, what natural sounds like and why it is popular, the overall mix and what brilliance it has but strength it contains at the same time through the EQ and mastering it has from high end frequencies to low end. You can hear how the singer sings and try to identify how the compressor is taken effect and if it is there in the first place. This may sound challenging to begin to do, but the more you do it the easier it gets and the more you hear. This is what makes a true Live Audio Mixer different from and amateur. You have to want it and be willing to practice it all the time.

4. Be willing to train your ears and hear in a way that you never thought you could before so that when it comes to show time you know what to listen for and know what sounds natural and know what that acoustic space will sound like. As I mentioned above, experience is your greatest teacher and every where you go you can be gaining experience. Constantly look for more to learn. No one has learned it all, and on the internet there are thousands and thousands of content to read and learn from. Get different views on the same thing and understand that to be successful in this business you have to apply yourself. Apart of the practice is taking criticism from others as mentioned before. This is not a space for you to be egotistic and think that you never everything because you will fail. Some of the best learning comes from criticism and you can't take it personally but instead it should inspire you to work even more and

become better. Always remember that in this industry there is an unlimited amount of competition. There is always going to be someone waiting to take your position, and the day that you stop learning is the day that you will end up losing your position that guy that worked harder than you.

Tools to Practice With

1. At this point you should understand that this it is a lifestyle to be a professional Mixer and that everything you hear is now you're learning space. With this there are also tools that can really help jumpstart your learning especially if you still just don't know exactly what to look for when it comes to frequencies or getting a good mix on a song. The best tool a Mixer can have would be a frequency generator. They have these as free apps on every smartphone for you to download and they are the perfect tools for a Mixer to begin to understand what to listen for frequency wise. Note that when using one on a phone's speaker about 180 Hz and lower and 7kHz and higher begin to really fade and may not be the right tone since the speaker is very weak. So what this gives you is a tool that produces frequencies best at the most audible range for humans to hear between about 180 Hz-7000 Hz meaning that you can practice the most important frequencies that are most noticeable any time you have your phone!

2. At least once a day you should whip out yo
   frequency generator app and just listen to
   different frequencies to begin to train your ear.
   The more you do this the better you'll get and
   your ear will start to expect a specific frequency
   sound coming out when you put the frequency
   generator at 400 Hz and are about to press
   play. When you feel comfortable enough, close
   your eyes and randomly pick a frequency and
   try to guess what it is based on what you hear.
   Do this for 2 minutes a day doing a range of
   frequencies and within a week or two you will
   begin to hear the difference and everything you
   hear. You will hear what stands out and why a
   sound may sound a certain way.

3. An example would be hearing the pilot talk
   through the speakers on the plane. He sounds
   so strange because he is missing all the low end
   from 120Hz up to 900Hz. With this ability you
   will be able to very quickly hear the anomalies
   in people's voices through microphones and
   instruments. Another great tool is to download
   an equalizer app for your phone. These allow
   you to control a range of frequencies for your
   music. So while your favorite song is playing,
   add a ton of 80Hz and you will hear how
   overpowering the bass is or do the opposite and
   reduce that frequency making it sound lifeless.
   Through this you can hear what sounds proper
   and what blends in the best. Professionals can
   be great teachers and listening to professionally
   done music will teach you what people like to
   hear and what mixes best. So when you use an
   equalizer app to ruin their perfect creation you
   will then understand their actions and intense
   when producing the music. This will allow you

to get the natural sound that you feel the audience should hear for live music. There are many other tools but these two are great starting points for any Mixer and are completely free and always accessible from your phone which is why they are perfect for all beginners.

Never Give Up

1. The last step in this guide is to never give up. To succeed in this world and what you love you have to truly respect and love what you do. It is no different in Live Audio Mixing and this is a lifestyle a majority of the world does not live. A majority of the world doesn't know that this really does exist and how much work goes into making the perfect show come alive. In this industry and with this job you will be beatdown by other people in times that you mess up or just don't have the experience yet, but way more often you will be beatdown by your own self. Many beginning Mixers go through rehearsals or situations where he or she is confused and does not know what to do. The absolute worst thing to do is to give up, but the second worst thing to do is make the situation worse by doing something completely wrong.

2. Everyone needs to understand that they are not perfect and that it is okay to ask questions. Maybe at the time it makes you look a little less professional whatever the question may be; however, it is better than making everything

worse and once you do your job during the show and prove that you are capable then no one looks at the question that was asked but hears that everything sounds good. It is a very stressful job with long hours for a short show most of the time and out of all your preparation you only have two hours to do your best. When things go wrong and you have an awful night you just cannot give up even if everyone blames you or no one does. And in this industry, as was mentioned earlier in the guide, when you do the best job you have ever done do not count on receiving any appreciation from anyone. You just have to understand that you did a great job and that is the type of show you expect yourself to run.

3. Opportunity is everywhere in this business and after you mess up whether it be once or even ten times you have to realize that your chances are not over yet and that you must learn from yourself. If you follow this guide you will greatly improve your opportunities of being successful and get you into position of doing what you love. This entire guide was written from experience and is what every single Mixer faces from the beginning to the end of his or her career. This is just a beginner's guide and there is so much more to learn but probably the two most important thesis of this job and for anyone in this industry is to absolutely use common sense and to never give up.

Recommended Resources

- HowExpert.com – Quick 'How To' Guides on All Topics from A to Z by Everyday Experts.
- HowExpert.com/free – Free HowExpert Email Newsletter.
- HowExpert.com/books – HowExpert Books
- HowExpert.com/courses – HowExpert Courses
- HowExpert.com/clothing – HowExpert Clothing
- HowExpert.com/membership – HowExpert Membership Site
- HowExpert.com/affiliates – HowExpert Affiliate Program
- HowExpert.com/writers – Write About Your #1 Passion/Knowledge/Expertise & Become a HowExpert Author.
- HowExpert.com/resources – Additional HowExpert Recommended Resources
- YouTube.com/HowExpert – Subscribe to HowExpert YouTube.
- Instagram.com/HowExpert – Follow HowExpert on Instagram.
- Facebook.com/HowExpert – Follow HowExpert on Facebook.

Manufactured by Amazon.ca
Bolton, ON

26160143R00026